*"Romanticisng our poems,
Eternalising our love."*

ROSES
ANTHOLOGY

ii PUBLISHING

ROSES Anthology

© 2020 Copyright of individual pieces remains with the contributors.

First published 2020

Copyright notice

All rights reserved. No part of this book may be reproduced in any form or by any electronic or mechanical means, including information storage and retrieval systems, without permission in writing from the authors or publisher.

Published by ii Publishing in conjunction with Poetix University

Cover design: tonii
Design and layout: Nupur Nair

Edited by Ahja Fox and Dara Kalima

ISBN: 978-1-7362167-1-2

Printed in the United States of America

iiPUBLISHING

New York, NY
www.toniiinc.com

"This love has no end or beginning. It exists freely."

CONTENTS

L	1
O	36
V	74
E	118
AUTHORS	210
INDEX	*218*

A Message from Our President

Love has carved a permanent place inside of poetry. From expressing the longing for a lover's touch to seranading a lover in sweet words, romantic poetry is a genre that is enjoyed by the world.

The ROSES anthology is a collection of poems created by poets from all around the world who partook in one of Poetix University's themed writing workshops. This particular one explored various aspects of romantic love. In this four-day workshop, students were asked, through uniquely crafted prompts, to express love inside their poetry. We explored romance poetically from the color red to Aphrodite, approaching love from various aspects. In this exploration, students were able to open their hearts and allow love to bloom like a rose.

So allow the words to bloom within you and watch love blossom in your mind. Share these words with your partner as your love resonates with the words expressed within these pages.

tonii
President of Poetix University

"Loving them"

"A manifestation of love, beauty, and fertility"

The seas seized silently
Yes, that's what it was to deaf ears that night
That night when its quake was violent enough to make
    sea creatures take flight

Seas seized violently
Yes, even deaf ears couldn't miss
An earth-shattering rumble originating from the
    seabed where lovers viciously kiss

Seas seized helplessly
And from its mouth foam came
And like all devastation, a measure of perfection
    came in exchange

Seas seized the shore
In desperation, releasing from the pit of its belly
A manifestation of love, beauty, and fertility

Seizures ceased
And now the seas could rest
Finding security and relief under
The fingertips of His sweet caress

"Aphrodite's Release"
Shana Bennett

"Romance blooms like a rose..."

Romance blooms like a rose,
Coming into my life making a home,
A passion I've never felt before,
A love I crave more and more.

You took my heart and took the pain away,
The passion burning day after day,
Love is as crimson as a redbird's wings,
Flying into the heavens making my heart sing.

You always know how to make me blush,
For your love, my heart will always gush,
I will always love you until death do us part,
You will always have my heart.

"Like A Rose"
James Dean Rivera

"My voice is poured into wine glasses..."

i. Supply
I serve myself willingly on every platter,
What a scrumptious spread I lay out,
Waiting for your heart to feast upon,
My voice is poured into wine glasses,
To help you wash down,
The spice of my thighs,
Thick and robust,
Building a lap,
Worthy to carry mountains,
Mountains of your pain,
So that we both may gain,
Some solace again.

ii. Demand
Your plate,
Although empty,
Does not satiate,
Your infinite appetite,
That is craving,
My caring,
My oversharing,
My blatant daring,

ii. Endless
Your smitten heart is revering,
So my love's kitchen,
Continues preparing,
Feast after feast,
In your honour it's grand,
Providing an indefinite,
Supply to your demand.

"Supply and Demand"
Nupur Nair

"It's two way; Highway, an expedition for love's sake."

Give or Take is what we do in the love we make.
It's two-way; Highway, an expedition for love's sake.
Trust, Commitment, Spontaneity, Honesty, and
    Loyalty are icing on that cake.
Plenty of fishes in the sea but we got hooked.
Hooked with the first bait we see; getting crooked.

Love takes time's surf around a bit; you haven't even looked.
Anticipation in the relationships with no gender, caste, age, nor creed.
Emotionally available for the better half without any greed.
Vulnerability and Compatibility as the common ground will make love eternally freed.

"Highway to Love"
Dhruvil Purani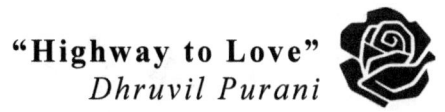

"Her lips manifested a cherry red crease..."

In her clueless language,
My eyes are looking for answers.
I'm flabbergasted by her dress,
Which is coated with a layer of scarlet.
Her scent breezed across me,
Like a basket of raspberries.
The moment she first saw me, I drowned in ecstasy,
Her eyes were as deep as the Atlantic, and long as the
    Arabian sea.
Her roaming, round eyes linger in my heart,
Even the fiery, red sun stands no chance to those
    eyes.

Her lips manifested a cherry red crease,
Drawing my attention towards her.
I heard my heart whisper, "She's the one!"
The way she brushed away her hair,
I fell into a pond of alluring beauty.
Her voice sings a melody in my heart,
Just like a cardinal.
She shone like a ruby,
And managed to pull my heartbeat towards her.
I knew at that moment that the spaces between her
      fingers were meant to be filled with mine.

"The Girl in Red"
Rithika

"I wear my finest Mars blush,

And proclaim my love..."

That cherry August morning,
Arrived like Christmas,
Knotting our hearts together,
With its autumn bows,

The butterflies in my stomach,
Are resurrected by your entrance,
Their wings fluttering voraciously,
Craving your flaming touch,

I wear my finest Mars blush,
And proclaim my love,
As you unravel my lips,
Sipping a scarlet kiss,

At this blooming moment,
Your fiery pulse confessed,
That ruby dice it had rolled,
Hoping to succumb to me,

Rejoicing at this perchance,
I feast on our romance,
Drenched in your rosy hue.
Savouring this red rendezvous.

"Red Rendezvous"
Nupur Nair

"To reach you was my ultimate goal."

The day I set my eyes on you,
They got stuck on you like a glue.
You gave me your love as a start,
In exchange, I gave you my heart.
We followed the actual barter system,
We teased each other and called it criticism.
Your lovely touch was my unlimited want,
And just your looks made me enchant.
Your warm hugs melt my soul,
To reach you was my ultimate goal.
You gave me your arms when I felt low,
Talked me out of the sorrows and made me glow.
You said "I love you" in many languages,
I'd never forget them at all, for ages.
You filled my life with happiness,
And gifted me a beautiful necklace.
You took me on a date in January,
And that was not just ordinary.
You took me to an amazing Yule ball,
Later, you walked me out of the hall.

We took a walk in the garden,
You knew I was really ardent.
You read me your beautiful poetry,
Under the shade of a banyan tree.
You hugged me under the moonlight,
Indeed, bringing me one nostalgic night.
You gave me my life's biggest surprise,
My stomach was filled with butterflies.
You knelt to the ground and pulled out a ring,
I said YES and we were passionately kissing.
You carried me in your arms and felt the moment,
You uttered the words "You're my bestowment"
You said to me that my wish was your command,
I felt that I finally satisfied my demand.
Every second of your time was what you supplied,
Infinite smiles on my face was what you applied.
You knew my every mood and curve,
No wonder, it is you who I'd always conserve.
I'd love you always forever and ever,
My wonderful and handsome lover.

"The Demand and Supply in our Love"
Rama Barathi

"He came very close to me

Without any physical touch."

He emerged in my life
As an angel in a nightmare.
Fascinated by his eyes,
I decided to care.

He made me obsessed with him
At the very first sight.
I fell in love
And I knew, I was right.

He stole my heart completely,
In a very short while.
And made me addicted
With his beautiful smile.

He came very close to me
Without any physical touch.
I wonder how can
I love a person this much.

My feelings for you rush
Like animals in herds.
How could I delineate you
In just words?

"My Romeo"
Chandini

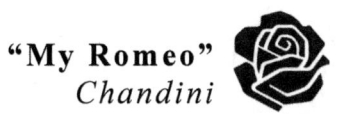

"Teared clouds arouse the fragrance of love."

Dancing in rain, feeling every drop,
Teared clouds arouse the fragrance of love.
Devouring every moment of the season,
Fulfilling our addiction to hopping potholes.
Abolishing the sorrows of dreadful spirits,
Fumbling our hearts making a soul connection.

This night is testing my patience,
Keeping me underneath with your passion.
Every reproduction of striking thunderbolts,
Makes feeling alive like a heart's cardiogram.
Never let you get flatlined dear,
You are eternal, nothing to fear.

"Shower of Love"
Dhruvil Purani

"Without you, I'm a mermaid who can't swim."

At first, we paddled by the bubbling edge;
the crackle of small pebbles singing sweet.
Seaweed strands between our toes did wedge
as hand in hand we followed flirting feet.

Once in, the water bathed us, and enthralled,
we merged into one body with the sea.
But as the sun set, land by tide's pull called
and you became detached, distant to me.

I trembled at the absence of my buoy,
trod water as the waves began to crash.
The passion of our unison dealt joy,
but now, alone, I sink beneath each splash.

With you, I felt my fear of life grow dim.
Without you, I'm a mermaid who can't swim.

"Lost, At Sea"
Sharron Green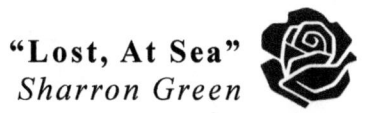

"Animosity abolished

Fulfillment flamed"

In that willing womb
Excellence exploded
And devoured demons
Simply with evidence of an embryo unlike any other

Animosity abolished
Fulfillment flamed
Patience poured
Passion powered
On

And
We were reborn
Into a promise
Reproduced
To reflect His face
We face
Another day
Only & all
Because of what took place
In that willing womb

"Willing Womb"
Shana Bennett

"The thought of her name always promised happiness to his heart."

They say love is a beautiful connection between two souls.
Unbreakable and unshakable it is
There are many such beautiful souls connected.
They have neither seen each other nor have spoken through mobile phones.
Letters exchanged from one to the other.
Their voices never spoke but their words did.
She sends him gifts wrapped in bright red, with love.
Which made him blush and his cheeks would turn as red as cherries.
The thought of her name always promised happiness to his heart.

Days passed...
Weeks passed......
Months passed.........
The special day came
They decided to meet
He wore a bright red suit while she wore a long red
    frock, embroidered with rose petals.
The moment they saw each other, they stood
    awestruck for a few moments.
Their hearts were filled with mixed emotions
He went on his knees and proposed to her
She was elated and jumped in joy
The red rose danced in the moonlight in his hands.

"Her Beauty in Red"
Rashmi

"The sight of you
Makes tectonic plates still"

It was fall
When they fell
Red
Juicy
Delicious
Desirable they were
And my stomach quaked
Tectonic plates shifted
Roaring for a taste
A bite of at least
One
Of those
Red
Juicy
Delicious
Apples
Falling
Into a basket with my name on it
He hands one to me, telling me to just go ahead and
        eat
No need to wait
Pick
One
Any
One
Because there is no *one*
Worth waiting for
He, snaggletooth, he
Hands me
One

Red
Delicious
Juicy
Is he

Stomach quakes
Earth shakes
Mouth watering
Should I wait?
Seasons change
Keep changing
Keep fading
Red to brown
Fading
Rotting
Stomach quaking
Everyone waiting
*There is no on*e, they say,
Just eat

Mouth opens
Saliva flooding the desert within
Snaggletoothed, mouth widens
Slowly
Eerily
In anticipation
For me to eat

Leaves fall
Reminding me of seasons changing
Time running
Maybe there *is* no *one*
Just many ripe for the picking
Lips press against the
Ripest
Juiciest
Apple I could pick
Like my 10-year-old lips used to press against my
    forearm to rehearse a kiss

Ready to eat
Because there is no *one* that can fill my stomach,
Any can do the trick
And snaggletooth agrees

And so I go
Ready to stop the quake with just one bite

And then
You...
Chocolate
Brown
Juicy
Delicious
You...

In my periphery
Under a different tree
Stand

Though blurry
I can see you coming in a hurry
And I am quickly reminded that red is not my color
And you
Not like the others

You, painted on my heart since I was 18, you
Who my stomach *truly quakes* for
You
Who I've dodged the fall of many apples for
You

The sight of you
Makes tectonic plates still
Growling cease
Winds chill
Hearts pieced
Together

Awe
Struck
Apple drops from my hand
And burns a hole in the sand
It was never mine to eat

I shift on the heels of my perspective to another tree
My name carved on it by *He*
And he
My he
My *one*
The *one*
That *no one*
Thought existed
Walks
No longer in my periphery

Eyes opened
Mouth shut
All stilled
And I am reminded of
My commitment
My conviction
My collection
Of a thousand
Letters
Dreams
Scenes
That don't include anyone but you

You, who will ignite my destiny, you
Who makes all logic cease, you
All math defied when
Your one
And my one
Make one

My love

It was fall

When I realized
You
Were the
Only *one* worth falling for

"It was Fall"
Shana Bennett

"He is my delectable delight and my culinary platter."

My love for him rests in the sturdiness of Twizzler
    licorice on my tongue.
Red and firm on the outside
With twisted spiral edges to denote the complexity of
    his inner being that no one else can feel but me.
My saliva moistens his razor-sharp edges
And the crimson undertone of my heartbeat plays
    Jazz beats with my veins and arteries whenever
    memories of him, coated like candy apples,
    enter my thoughts.
He is my delectable delight and my culinary platter.
His spirit tastes like red velvet cupcakes, full of
    calories, but I don't mind the weight gain.
He feeds me his heart like a cold slice of watermelon
    on a hot summer's day.

I love him beyond the crimson that runs through my
    frame.
No traffic signal in red
Or blazing fire truck at night
Could douse this flame that burns so bright.
Culinary and candy is he for me
Because he sees my Soul and enters deep.
To feed me,
To tease me,
To love me,
Beyond my red fingernails
Or red painted lips,
He loves me for me
And I love him for him—the sweetest desserts one
    could ever eat.

"Culinary & Candy"
Taneeka L. Wilder

"Ragged over rules of blood,
Lke Romeo did with Juliet."

Lost in your blushing body,
As red bugs plant bait.
Ragged over rules of blood,
Like Romeo did with Juliet.
Raw as ruddy passion fruit,
I would suck over your rosy brims.
Relinquished waving red hairs,
Caressing my face, salving cream.

Dine over soft red velvet cheeks,
Walking over cherry blossom streets.
Relished reference of the pink brain,
Raging rubicund garnet eyes meet.
Liaison of our reverence never seen,
Waltz over melodies in a red silk gown.
Laying underneath a lucky blood moon,
Ruling over my heart with a smile as a crown.

"Red Love"
Dhruvil Purani

"Open-heartedly"

"O rdained the Goddess of True love"

A castaway propelled to sea
P apa castrated dreadfully
H er body from his foam did rise
R evered for beauty, laughing eyes
O rdained the Goddess of True Love
D olphin a symbol, also a dove
I n art, depicted nude and proud
T he fertile message, fanfare loud
E mbodiment of well-endowed

"APHRODITE"
Sharron Green

"For love and passion, you turned the light on."

Goddess of love, fertility, and beauty,
Born from the foam of the sea,
Daughter of Zeus and Dionne—
For love and passion, you turned the light on.

Love that lifts me to the heights of Mount Olympus.
The spirit of love is always with us,
So powerful and divine,
Always gets better with time.

You fill me up with love and I'm never full,
Always showing that magnetic lure at full pull.
Sucking me into a vortex of love and romance,
Love I'll always appreciate and study never at a
      glance.

And I do believe in love and I can attest,
And in my lovers arms, I'll always rest.
Feeling safe and committed hearts intertwined,
Captured by the powerful spell of Aphrodite's spell
      divine.

"Aphrodite's Power"
James Dean Rivera

"We'll grant each other time's kisses
And create a world of lore"

If I could, I'd lay in the sky
Watch the magic of the sea foam rise
Bear witness to the birth of beauty
And fall deep into the trance of her eyes

It's here where solace is found
When the ramblings of the world contort
The vision of my future and of my past
Where rest finally finds my heart

Walk the coastlines with me, Aphrodite
Let's leave our love in the sand
The dark origins of your birth will help you
Learn how to further expand

We'll teach each other the secrets
Of an intimate kind of adore
We'll grant each other time's kisses
And a create a world of lore

Oh Aphrodite...

If I could, I'd become the shore
Where your sea foam crashes in
Where your lips would softly take form
Across this expanse of passion

"Aphrodite: An Ode"
Sarrah Safi

"Intense passion

Seeking to burn up in flames"

We seek fulfillment
Finding our match in another human being

Wanting to be devoured
Kept safe within the arms of our lovers

Intense passion
Seeking to burn up in the flames

Such undertaking will require patience
A desire to stay, to intertwine

You'll have to abolish your fear
Love is terrifying, an unknown gamble

There will never be a reproduction
The same love will not come twice

"Leap of Faith"
Michaela Jean

"...my blood was circulating faster,
My pulse pulsating higher..."

I still remember the day I saw you;
It was the month of Valentine.
I was entering into the coffee shop,
The clock hit the time nine.
Seeing everyone giving roses,
Spending time with their love,
Except for me, everyone was looking fine.

A cool breeze touched my face,
My eyes stuck at the gate.
Saw you for the first time,
My heartbeat started racing,
Lyrics of love, I started humming
Music I could feel without a base.

Your scintillating red dress.
The lips, having the red shades,
The essence of a rose petal.
The cheeks looked like a strawberry.
Brighter than the diamond, your eyes shined.
Your fingers like a rose velvet...
To give you happiness and be in your life;
I wanted to be your only Man.

Red color, I always thought of as a sign of danger.
But that day, I came to know
It's the symbol of love.
When my blood was circulating faster,
My pulse pulsating higher,
It was the beginning of an unrequited love—
My mind and heart, you enrapture.

"Love in Red, Unrequited Love"
Mahesh Maheshwari

"Won't you come back to fill the colours in me?"

Love is a memory which no one can steal
But it can leave scars which no one can heal.
My gloomy days
Were turned into dreamy ones by you.
I'm now just a plain painting without your presence,
Won't you come back to fill the colours in me?
Your voice echoes in my mind all day long,
Without you, my days seem to prolong.
I wanna place my head on your shoulders
And feel the breath of you on me one more time.
I wanna take a stroll on the shore of the beach,
Clutching your hands,
Ditching away my worries,
Fetching your love for me one more time.
I wanna suck the love you have for me outta you,
Just like an insect which sucks honey.
I wanna cuddle up close to you
And watch a romantic movie
Along with the glimpse of that blushing face of yours
      one more time.

Our relationship is a growing plant
In which I'm the shoot
And you are the root of my life.
O love, have you forgotten my love for you?
Are you tired of my care for you?
I miss your voice which sings a melody in my ears.
I miss your tight hugs which allowed the
      synchronisation of our souls.
I miss the way you care for me,
I drown in my tears
Filled with your memories.
I'm breaking into pieces over and over again,
Which are filled with your sophisticated grace.
My love! It gets harder, every minute,
To pretend I don't go through anything.
But I hope you can still see the truth
Through my fruitful eyes.
And I still wait for you to rescue me
From this continuing bondage of pain!

"Since You Left"
Rithika

"You would not enter my mind constantly,

but when you did, you devoured."

I saw the passion in your pleading brown eyes,
in your coarse hands and the way they
reached, rubbed, and embraced mine.
It was never your intention to abolish our friendship,
but simply, to add onto it.
Patience, deeply instilled, a blessing and a curse,
but as you said, *it's better to start off friends,*
    anyway.

The fulfillment in my own life began falling into
    fruition.
You would not enter my mind constantly,
but when you did, you devoured.
And the truth is, the reproduction of anyone else
filling that space was impossible.

And then I knew...

"Untitled #1"
Michel M. Antoine
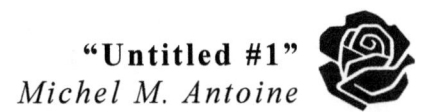

"Eyes reflecting unsaid feelings

Emotions dipped in passion"

An actor in this play of love
Portraying my own character
Eyes reflecting unsaid feelings
Emotions dipped in passion
A longing to share proximity
A spot beside you on red carpet
A contact in your priority folder

Shoulder for you to rely on
Made some cuts to fit in
The frame they set up for love
Played my part with commitment
With each take of a clapping board
I was playing your protagonist
But in the pages of your script
My role—just a supporting cast

"Supporting Actor"
Tejashri Pathak

"I miss being unable to breathe while you devour me with your lips."

Without you, my life has no meaning at all,
I listen to songs and find no music in them,
I take my guitar and its strings are missing,
I try to read a book,
But the pages have nothing written,
I feel like a lonely book on the rack,
The clouds have faded from the sky,
The ocean has dried up,
The greens have given up on their lives,
There's no pure oxygen left,
The nights don't bring me moon and stars,
It feels like an end of the world, without you.

I am empty inside and life is hopeless,
No distance will keep me away from you,
My every moment will pass through you,
Everything reminds me of your brilliant face;
I write countless poems about you.
You're as shining as a twinkling star,
But they aren't as bright as you are.
I wish I could light up the sky again,
Talk to the stars and spell your name;
I wish I could see the past us again,
So that I could go fall in love all over again.

Take us back to the place where we were before,
Take us back to who we used to be—
The time when we were very happy,
Take us back to that beautiful night,
When you held me so tight,
Take us out of this sorrow,
Let's travel every now and tomorrow.

Take us back to the moment we kissed,
When the bright star shined for us,
Take us back to the time,
Where your love was as strong as
Unbreakable armour,
Take me into your heart, I would wash away all the pain,
Take me into your heart, I would never rip it apart.

I miss being unable to breathe while you devour me with your lips.
I miss the way you used to look at me with a sense of wanting.
I miss you, I miss us, I miss myself.
I often talk to the star—that wherever you are, our love shall win,
Without any flaw or grin, I will keep loving you and missing you,
My eyes are silent, my smile so fake, without you in my life.

I love you a lot!
Please come back, my boy.
I miss us a lot!
Come back to me; let's create new memories,
Let's heal our scars and broken hearts,
I need my heart to beat again.
Come back to me, can we restart?

"Come Back To Me, My Love"
Rama Barathi

"Love turned to hurt, transformed into starlight"

Can't breathe
Can't think
All-consuming loss robs me blind

A flash of light
A deafening boom
A deer caught in headlights

Our time wasn't supposed to be so limited
So much still to happen
Oh how I wish you could see love's dreams

Discordant music floods my mind
I need you here
Fervent wishes left unheard

I love you seems so small now
Unworthy of the feelings coursing through my veins
Can you hear me?

Cries of agony filled my nights
Grief is powerful but time is master of all
The hurt fades

Fond memories surface
Laughter floats through open windows
Love turned to hurt, transformed into starlight

Can you hear me?
I wish you were here again
But wishes are for magic lamps

"Don't Deny the Reaper"
Michaela Jean

"The shadows of the past seem Brighter than the future"

When all certainty is taken away
It is not an easy feeling
It sends your stomach in a spin
It triggers racing *What ifs*

This is where the devil plays
Toying with every emotion
Attached to these thoughts of losing and loss
In a heart that's freshly broken

Oh, the anger we muster
The tears that spill freely
The wishes we make as we
Contemplate weakly

Somehow
No fantasy suffices
To the laughter we've shared together
Somehow
The shadows of the past seem
Brighter than the future

Our love is certainly stronger than this
I've seen its flames in your eyes
We help each other find meaning
Without a façade or disguise

Let's turn this mess into memories
Let's forget the in-betweens
Let's go back to how things were
Before we tore apart our dreams

"Rewind"
Sarrah Safi

"Vortex of thoughts encumbered me

The shadow of our love I can still see"

Am I still dreaming
Or is it a nightmare
Or it's now my reality
When I saw here and there
I didn't find you near

I'm so lost in your memories
Vortex of thoughts encumbered me
The shadow of our love I can still see
Every breathe without you I'm taking
My life is now a curse for a living

From dusk to dawn
No one I know except you in the whole town
How much I love you
Not able to recite
Every place we visited
I see the reflection of memories inculcated

I just want you to be back
I don't want to strangulate myself with the shack
I will die if you will not come
You're my only reason to live
It was a bad phase now it's gone
Baby come again it's my only wish

I'm incomplete without you
Traces of pain and the shadow of death I can see
I just want to have a life with you
Without you I have no reason to live
I just know I want you back
I love you

"Untitled #2"
Mahesh Maheshwari

"Though writing was my passion I couldn't find words to describe that moment"

I was in deep sorrow
Sitting in a cafe in isolation
I saw him
He devoured me completely, just with those almond
    eyes
The sight of him abolished all my disparity and
    sorrow
My heart was pounding and was reproductively
    beating

I lost all my patience
Though writing was my passion
I couldn't find words to describe that moment
I wasted no more time
I felt I would attain my fulfillment in his heart
I went to him and explained everything; what I felt
      from my heart
He was flabbergasted
Thereby, his soul got adhered to mine

"When I Saw Him..."
Rashmi

"Looking into your loveless eyes, I'm half killed."

We came closer,
Fell in love with each other,
And it went smooth.
Suddenly, I realised
A gap between us
Due to the lack of your efforts.
I felt remorse,
For falling in love.
Then I fell into
Fear's deepest curve;
Yes, the fear of losing you.
It'd happen someday, I knew,
And now the day is here,
I'm trapped into a pain
That no one can cure.
Loving you deeply
Was the only mistake I made;
Looking into your loveless eyes,
I'm half killed.
You threw me out of your life,
I felt like someone pierced
Deep into my heart
With a sharp knife.
You went very far away;
Praying for your happiness
Is the only thing I do everyday.

I've lost the precious treasure of my life
And that's you.
If you'd at least miss me or not,
I really don't have a clue.
Without you,
I'm living like a plain sky
Without stars;
Baby, please come back
To heal all my scars.
Trying to throw away your memories,
But my heart can't cope.
You'll come back to me
With the same love one day, I hope.
The way you loved you,
The way you protected me,
The way you cared for me,
The way you touched my soul,
Got amalgamated
With my blood and flesh.
I miss you a lot!
Please come back my dear,
Let's start it fresh.
I still couldn't perceive
In what way I was wrong;
But the one thing
I need you to know is that,
I love you,
I will love you and only you
For life long.

"My Broken Soul"
Chandini

"A patient tempo of emotions

Dipped in shades of blue

As I rhythmically play the chords"
In an attempt to abolish
Traces of heart-aching anguish
Devouring me like a demon
I let my fingers seek solace
In the monochrome keys

Passion running from my fingertips
Fulfilling each moment of ecstasy
A patient tempo of emotions
Dipped in shades of blue
As I rhythmically play the chords
Lost in the world of notes trying
To reproduce our love melody

"Monochrome Keys of Love"
Tejashri Pathak

"From caterpillars to butterflies, We fly."

If we knew then what we know now—that love tastes different when it is cooked in healing and baked with selflessness
No longer would we have to shrink ourselves to prove our validation
Or think that we are not enough in order to appease another's Ego.
No longer would we have to cower and shrink beneath the dermis of our skin to ease another's insecurities, fears, and projections.

To know that we are more than enough,
To know that we are whole,
To know that love is as natural and free and accepting
    of thee,
To know that love costs nothing...because it only asks
    you to BE,
Is a complete experience beyond mere definition.
We grow.
Grow for each other and ourselves.
The best of friends,
The best of lovers,
Nurturing a Home in each other,
Beyond habit and comfort,
From caterpillars to butterflies,
We fly.
In love.
By first being Love itself.

"The Message"
Taneeka L. Wilder

"Valuing them"

"As all the earthen vessels made by the potter end up in being broken..."

Love is, expecting the unexpected
You were always there for me
We both never ever felt that to love is a duty
It was like oxygen and water, it was for us
We both stood for each other at all times, and faced
      all the obstacles to attain our destiny

Your presence vanishes all my worries like grime
Your hugs and kisses on my forehead always
      comforts me
I am an obedient baby crawling behind you
You were a dream for which I would sleep all days

But it happened...

As all the earthen vessels made by the potter end up
   in being broken,
So is the life of mortals
All humans fall in the hands of death and are subject
   to death
You went away from me, to a place where I can't
   come
Without you and your presence my life turned hollow,
   hopeless, and haggard
Please come back to me, I am still not able to take in
   the acrid truth of your long sleep

"Where Did You Go?"
Rashmi

"...love never leaves its home, but the home it does leave—it was not meant to live in—"

I cannot think of any moment in time
Where I pleaded for love to take me back and honor
    me like a succulent goddess,
To value me like copper clinging to a penny
Or to regard me like fans cheering for their favorite
    celebrity.
Like a thirsty child begging for water,
My parched tongue could never be quenched.

By the mathematics of a love obsessed with
    subtraction & division.
Deep wisdom and ever-growing maturation have
    taught me that love never leaves its home, but
    the home it does leave—it was not meant to
    live in—with no mortgage and no damn rent to
    send in.
So, the love that lost me was also responsible for
    finding me. It taught me that there is no
    greater love than that which resides within the
    depths of me.

"Lost Love I Say Not"
Taneeka L. Wilder

"Steeled heart sucked into the sea monster that was my present..."

The sun packed her bags and exited stage left for an
    extended vacation
Lawn mower over the bed of roses in my heart,
    devouring every last stem like a midnight snack
One petal survives the attack
It lives
To drown
In rivers of tears that would lead to seas if not
    stopped

Steeled heart sucked into the sea monster that was my
    present
There was no future
Deeper and Deeper it took me
Pressure on my chest like a violent hand holding me
Down
Intending me to drown
It took me
Deeper
Blurry Blue
Misty Midnight
Pitch
Black
Conscience kidnapped
I've lost myself
Lost just about every feeling
Except—

The feeling of braided fiber around my waist
Hold on, hang on, I hear bubbling faintly in my ears
Body limp and yet I feel a slight pull
Up
Conscience gone but I can faintly hear what sounds
    like someone saying, *hold on*
Higher and higher my limp body is propelled
Out

Flat surface rests gently under my body, I feel
Pumps to the chest
Familiar lips press
Fiercely against mine and breathe air into my semi-
    lifeless body
I see two ways out:
One where rays stab through dark spaces, spoiler
    alerting the sun's sharp U-turn back to its
    position,
The other where eternal emptiness meets eternal end
    and darkness dances the tango with
    demons
The former, no clear promises that the route will be
    easy but a clear way through
The latter, ends the misery quick and easy
A clear way out
Dark clouds of smoke interweave with my fingertips
    as I hold my hand out
To the easier way out and I—

Heart paused

Hold on, her raw honey sweet voice pleads as she
    administers rhythmic pumps of hope to my
Body

And I

Chose to listen
To the girl who stood over me
Radiant, beautiful, rose
Recognizable she seemed
Brilliant she was

And I
Chose to give it another go and
Dance a cha-cha with the rays once again
Into my mouth she sent breath from her vessel to
    mine and I
Inhaled
And like an IV rushing through my veins
Peace ran rampant through my being
Tingling sensations in my toes
And I
Heard my heart begin to beat a drum
Steady and rhythmic was he

And she
Faded
Into the light at a different part of my course
Seemingly assuming her rightful place

And I
Chose to hold on
To the beautiful rose that is, was, and always will be,
    me

"Daring to Resuscitate"
Shana Bennett

"I was hungry for a dream convinced he was a genie."

I couldn't even remember the fight.
Maybe there wasn't one.
Maybe you just slowly disappeared like the way
    snowflakes do on my tongue.
I couldn't communicate the words
I don't deserve this.
I deserve to be treated like royalty,
like the Queen I know I am to be.
But all I could think was
if not him, who? If not him...me?
Couldn't be...
So, I drove an hour upstate with barely putting
my foot or mind on the brake and told myself
"I think I'm crazy. We haven't talked in weeks."
It seems that's what emotional abusers do.
Convince you you're the one that's crazy.
You start acting all jealous, not sure how
you landed on this ugly place called rage in the first
    place.
He called on my way up, asked if I wanted to hang
    out.
"Yes...but did you know I was coming?"
(Once again, not knowing then that
I was advocating for my own existence).
"Yeah," he said nonchalantly, "mom told me."
I was on this rollercoaster back then.
Fighting for a love that never existed.
Falling in the pitfalls of promises of family and
marriage, getting blamed whenever there was
    distance.
I was hungry for a dream convinced he was a genie.
I used to pray to God to give me a sign that this was
    all wrong.
That he would just fuck up and leave me alone.

It's called fear.
I didn't know it then.
When you feel stuck, and alone, and scared to leave
you find answers to questions that exist
but are not yet spoken out loud and you believe
you are the culprit of everything bad.
It's called fear. And abuse.
I tried to reclaim our relationship that day but
again he took the blame and placed it in my hands
as his tears rolled down claiming I was too good for
    him.
Why is that bad, one might ask.
Because... when your thoughts and actions are
completely devoured by what he would say or
think before your own...
When everything from what you wear to
what you eat to who you talk to becomes
an afterthought only after you've considered his
    needs...
When the inconsistency becomes consistent of
his bullshit excuses of disappearing like a bunny
with no magic show then you know.
It wasn't right.
It wasn't love.
I was driving myself crazy.
But he had the wheel, the gas, the transmission.
He was driving me crazy.
His name was ***...

"Driving Myself Crazy"
Michel M. Antoine

"It was our home,
Before and after we got lost."

We learn to love,
Before we can speak the word.

For it does not run on speech,
But on the notion of freedom,
Taking pit stops at lust town,
On cheat days.

It was our teacher,
Before we were students.

Making us practice self-love,
Distributing it selflessly,
Recycling negative energies,
Transforming them into growth.

It was a pandemic,
Before pandemics were real.

It feeds on acceptance,
Widely spread among empaths,
Getting caught on their smiles,
Acting before speaking.

Love was a healer,
Much before pain met us.

Harming our trauma,
By numbing its side effects,
Through spiritual connections,
Oblivious to boundaries.

It was our home,
Before and after we got lost.

We must put down,
The overweight baggage,
Rest our spines,
And settle down here.

Because...
My friend,
Love was
And forever will be,

Enough.

"What is 'Love'?"
Nupur Nair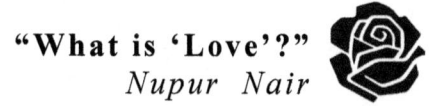

"Exuding insatiable desires, expelled from the blood in her heart..."

The Most Beautiful of them all,
Her companions adorned her with apples resting on
    beds of rose petals.
Aphrodite, Goddess of Ares and Eros,
Exuding insatiable desires, expelled from the blood in
    her heart;
Born from the flames of passion, created
From two emotionally-imbalanced parents.
Whatever she coveted, she could've had it,
Including many lovers she acquiesces.

Charming her consorts with seductive language,
Her chastisement left victims in anguish.
She was shameless, an established harlot;
A well-known whore who managed brothels.
Her contribution, a delicate balance of lust and love
While married she philanderers flexing, twisting
    smooth as a dove.
Reciprocity she sows, as above as is below
Is what we reap; (society)
Thirsty for love's poisonous concoction an eternal
    dance of bitter and sweet.

"The Most Beautiful of Them All"
LaDasha-Diamond

> "Planting a new garden
>
> Decorating my soul as you begged my pardon"

You say you love me
Can't you see
How all this breaks my heart
Tearing us apart

We had a love so strong
They were jealous and wrong
Crying every night
Missing you holding me tight

This darkness makes me hide
Wishing I had you by my side
I promise to love you 'til the end of time
Hoping you would only be mine

All I have are these tears
Plus, what we've experienced these past years
Your betrayal is an erupting volcano
Asking how I'm feeling, no Bueno

Pain revisiting our life
Don't forget, I'm still your wife
Take my tears away
Contemplating whether you can come home to stay

My emotions are like the colors of a rainbow
I need you to continue being my beau
I'm trying to be brave like a lion
Daring to test your waters and retreat to Zion

Many told me to leave you
You know deep down that would make me blue
Don't forget the meaning of "I do"
It means *through thick and thin*, there will always be
    a me and you

Big empty space
Only you can replace
Our life is like a thorny rose
Not perfect, but perfect for each other, only God
    knows

Seeing the regret in your eyes
Part of my heart forgives your lies
It matters how hard you try
Despite it causing me to breakdown and cry

My life is like a rollercoaster
Your constant asking for forgiveness, brings me
    closer
Your mouth and actions contradicted your heart
Look how far we've drifted apart

Now I reminisce about you night and day
Hanging on to every word you say
All I keep seeing is selfishness and arrogance
Let's not forget ignorance
This must be a final test
Making me feel like I'll always be second best
You said you cared about all our dreams
Yet all I can hear are my inner screams

I've been considering building back our stability and trust
Giving us a second chance is feeling like a must
I pray that one day you will see
That I never needed you, as much as you needed me

Music to my ears
Listening to you bare your soul of fears
Apologizing for how you stunted our family tree
Realizing honesty is key

My ego won't hurt
Confessing I will always love you, feeling extrovert
Ready to turn a new page
Part two to our book, as we engage

I'm letting go of this feeling, that our system was hacked
Most of our files corrupted and ransacked
An update needed
Battery recharging, because it overheated

Downloading an antivirus
Preventing future bugs from contaminating our siris
Time to stop focusing on pain
Let's refocus on the gain

I'm ready to cherish a new bond
Waiting on you to respond
The door to my heart is still open
Nervous is what I'm feeling as I reopen

Deep wounds magically healing
Welcoming you back, perfectly sealing
Learning painful lessons
The power of love and forgiveness our greatest
    blessings

Planting a new garden
Decorating my soul as you begged my pardon
Our love is like a never-ending story
About two people who survived every category

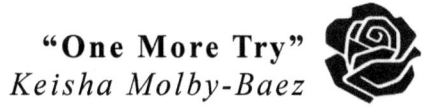

"One More Try"
Keisha Molby-Baez

"For some love is an education, If they knew they'd be in a better place..."

Love is not always a fairytale and it doesn't fall on your feet,
Love doesn't always come at first sight with the first person you meet,
Most people don't know what love means,
Not enough understanding of the love they need.

Sometimes there's no love language, no communication,
For some love is an education,
If they knew they'd be in a better place,
But sometimes heartbreak they constantly face.

There will sometimes be rejections and broken
    promises,
And there will be hurt and awfulness,
Your feelings may not be reciprocated,
And it'll make you feel irritated.

But with the right person through hard work,
You can have a love that shows more than worth,
It can take months, it could take years,
But love will one day come, have no fear.

"Two Conversations"
James Dean Rivera

"Cherries blossom in the spring but you popped our first kiss in the winter."

We stared into each other's eyes as if it was the first time,
the way a mother tends to a lost child,
protectively but not familiarly,
we crossed unchartered waters.
As our lips landed onto one another's like
love-budding hands first interlocking,
we welcomed it.

It felt sweet but we took our time to
bite into it like strawberries.
There was no need for extra sugar
as the years we built into a secured friendship
had then satisfied our now-aching hunger
for more.
We compromised our friendship for a kiss
knowing it could take a whirlwind in
the dynamic of our relationship.

Relationship-wise, we had a lot to learn.
If kisses led to signs, a stop sign wouldn't have made it in.
Like rain falling on drying clothes outside,
we submersed ourselves into what we knew
would only feel better on the other side.
Each side of us, our left, right, front, back,
all eight sides coming together.
Pulling us closer, meshing,
like the sound of a fire truck siren as it gets closer.
Closer to safety.
Closer to home.

Home sweet home, your lips told me.
One would think with the good luck that sprinkled on
        us,
the way rain falls on blooming flowers,
or rainfalls answering drought's questions,
that we were drizzled in ladybugs.
Each one with the strength of a lion
because I swore this wouldn't be the first.

First time for everything,
even something like this.
Cherries blossom in the spring but
you popped our first kiss in the winter.
There was no blood nor trail of shame
for something we both wanted.
But wanting and needing are two different things.

Things.
Things.
Things that are red...
A juicy strawberry in the shape of a kiss.
A stop sign... nowhere in sight.
A fire truck with you as my safety.
A ladybug reminding me I'm home.
A cherry popping. No blood at hand.
I'm not seeing red. I only see you.
Wanting and needing are indeed two different things.
We're both different
so let's settle
on both.

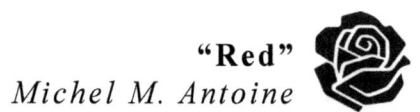

"**Red**"
Michel M. Antoine

"She is my love, my muse, my rose."

At first glance, romance bloomed,
It was red, not black with gloom,
Brown eyes that hypnotize,
My feelings for her were out of sight.

I fell in love with her from the first moment,
I knew she had feelings for me and she showed it,
The passion pierced through my soul,
To make her mine, I gave it my all.

I love her deeply, she loves me deeply,
And it's such a great feeling,
She is irreplaceable no one will come close,
She is my love, my muse, my rose.

When she became mine, I felt like a champ,
My love was elevated up a high ramp,
Love blooms like a rose,
Soon we'll be betrothed.

"At First Glance"
James Dean Rivera

"The serene splendour of a dying sun"

The flash, flirt of a Sevillanas' swirl
The cut, shine of a ruby ring
The blaze, crackle of an inferno
The deep velvet of a Chianti
The passion, thrust of a volcano
The timeless serenity of a rose
The soft vibrancy of a robin's breasts
The bubble, gush of arterial blood

The triumphant fanfare of Autumn leaves
The patent pride of a ladybird
The resolute rust of ancient rock
The 'seize the day' of a butterfly's wing
The 'you've been warned' wink of a danger sign
The serene splendour of a dying sun
The heroic sacrifice of a poppy

"Love in Red"
Sharron Green

"Illuminated with beauty, and kissed bronze by the sun..."

Once upon a time,
About six hours ago,
A rumble happened in the East Bronx,
And it was quite a show.
Venus rose out of the Bronx River
From a sperm induced foam,
Scaring some of its residents because they saw this as
    a freak show.
Illuminated with beauty, and kissed bronze by the
    sun,
One young man recognized her and yelled, "Yooo!
    That's Afro!"
In a soft mellow voice, she started to sing
And spoke with such eloquence, Bronx News 12 had
    to record the whole scene.
"I've come to bring you blessings, and I've come to
    show you lessons.
I've come to help you calm your rumbling inner sea,
    and I've come this spring harvest to assist
    you in planting new seeds."

As she continued to speak,
Every eye was transfixed
At how such beauty could exist in the Bronx
As it did not make any sense.
Noting their consternation, she told them to look
 toward the stars,
To see their faces in Venus and Mars.
To see their storms travelling alongside Poseidon's
 traces,
To be slow to avenge and take up arms as this shadow
 exists,
But to also recognize the beauty that lies within.
She reminded them that they were also planets too,
Castrated from their true nature and Divine
 destinations.
So, with this brief visit that caused a stir,
This side of the Bronx was changed to start a ripple
 throughout the world.
And for once in their lives,
The people became awakened,
By this goddess called "Afro",
That brought them back to recreating Planet Earth
 with love, beauty, and patience.

"Aphrodite: A Bronx Tale"
Taneeka L. Wilder

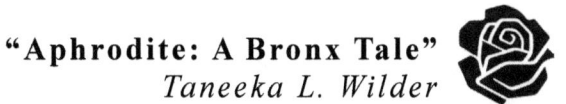

"Magical muse collecting hearts,
And yet, settled in none..."

My foaming lady,
Hatched from heaven,
Cradled by the arms of many,
And yet, held by none,

My rose syruped goddess,
With waves in her hair,
Delivering cupids,
And yet, mothering none,

My golden apple,
Broken for fertility,
Sensing their oceanic thirst,
And yet, quenching none,

My swan perched damsel,
Gliding through a posterity,
Magical muse collecting hearts,
And yet, settled in none,

My saintly aphrodisiac,
Sprinkled on their ardour,
Leaving them breathless,
And yet, satisfied by none,

My Aphrodite,
They tried to fit you into stone,
Tried to translate your curves,
But tasted war in your nerves,
And were conquered yet again.

My harmonious Love Queen,
You live among the galaxies,
Reigniting all the stars,
Every time they fall.

You are not mine,
You are not theirs,
You are yours.

"Yours"
Nupur Nair

"My love for him is like painting a red cross, symbolizing my love is his medicine and his mine"

His love is like a red apple in season all the time
My love for him is like cherries in my Mai Tai,
    incomplete without his love

He is my red marker, the one I use to outline the best
    moments of my life
My love for him is like the circle of eternity, forever
    his

My love for him is like a shot of coconut rum, making
    him feel good all the time
My love for him is a whirlwind romance, carried away
    by his passion

He is like my favorite red scarf, a lucky charm and
    cherished forever
My love for him is like a road map, telling what we've
    been through and where we're going

My love for him is like a shield, protecting him from
    all negativity and evil
He is the other half of my heart

My love for him is intoxicating, drunk on deep caring
    emotions
His kiss is like eating a red starburst, mouthwatering
    and sweet

My love for him is like my favorite songs, melodies,
    and tunes to soothe his soul
My love for him is like a painting filled with red
    roses, expressing unconditional appreciation

His words are a fire burning with care and kindness
My love for him is like a double scoop of pistachio
    ice cream, delicious and eager to devour

His touch is like handcuffs, tying up my hands and
    opening my legs
My love for him is like painting a red cross,
    symbolizing my love is his medicine and his
    mine

His cooking skills is a nutrient for my health
I love him like a dog loves his bone

My love for him is an absolute knockout, falling
    helplessly with desire
I love him like a pet loves their treats

My love for him is a captured sunset, where the
    warmth never grows dim
I love him like an actor loves their script

My love is a bright light making him feel special
My love for him is like a red blanket, keeping him
    warm through the rainy storms

His love making skills is like my pomegranate and
    cinnamon candle, burns slowly calming my
    nerves
My love is lightning to his thunder and the sunshine
    to his storm

His laughter is music to my soul
My love is a red carpet for his dreams

My love for him is like a river of understanding and
    blessings, once in it he doesn't want to leave
His smile is sunshine to my life

My love for him is like a box full of red gems,
    valuable and rare
My love for him is like a stage, to highlight all his
    great qualities

I love him like the moon loves the night sky
My love is a red lamp, the light that can get through everything dark

My love for him is like a tulip, opening to the warmth of Spring
His voice is the love birds chirping in my ear, mesmerizing sounds I enjoy

My love for him is like magic, no one can break the spell but him
My love for him is complete desire in the heart, spreading into his soul

His tongue is a red paintbrush, swiping across the middle section of my canvas
My love for him is a poem, a poem my pen will forever adore

I love him like a hungry man loves his food
I love him like his penis loves my pussy

I love him like a model loves their looks
I love him like an author loves writing books

"Hot Sand On My Beach"
Keisha Molby-Baez

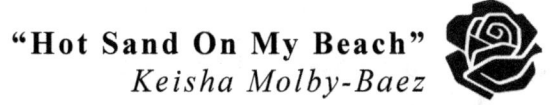

"Allowance for primal hunger devours any division."

Passion filled kisses usher in our introduction;
As fulfillment is achieved through mutual seduction.
Both lovers abolish all inhibitions,

Allowance for primal hunger devours any division.
It is through our intuition we witness the inner
 wisdom;
We envision reproduction creating a new beginning.
Yes, at life, we are winning.

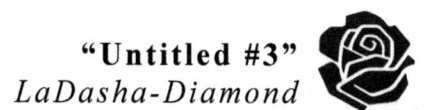

"Untitled #3"
LaDasha-Diamond

"Every moment"

"Sweet like ripe rasberries

Your sun-speckled sweat"

Your sexy slithering
Sneaks static through my skin
A pulse of red quickening

I didn't know I had this much blood
The steam of our touch
Alluring

Sweet like ripe raspberries
Your sun-speckled sweat
Beaded across your brow
Beckoning for more now

Our spirits shake synergy
Our doubts decompose
The petals of our passion
Bloom like a rose

"Sensation"
Sarrah Safi
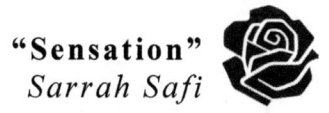

"A warmth was born in your touch, It was hot as lava but surprisingly warm."

You're a Magnificent handsome mystery.
If you ask me to describe you, where will I start?
I can't possibly fathom my thoughts into words
And turn you into a description of art.
Your eyes; like the shooting stars,
Your lips; a drug I should abstain,
Your laugh; a hilarious demeanor,
Your heart; like an earthquake making me run to you,
Your words are my poetry, entrapping me.

I had you hooked with my boldness and courage.
Your soul is my purity, your smile is my serenity;
A warmth was born in your touch,
It was hot as lava but surprisingly warm.
Your scent is like a sweet alyssum—
The peace in your voice and safety in your arms.
You're impossible to describe,
Rarer than a white peacock;
You're my mystery!

"My Mystery Man"
Rama Barathi

"Each thorn plucked with care

Keeping thou safe from prickle"

An early morning surprise
Rose bouquet on ordinary day
A note tucked in the middle
Words never been my métier
They, thy proficient territory
All I possess are emotions
Stuck within tight sealed lips

Single red rose inadequate
To convey the depth of love
Each thorn plucked with care
Keeping thou safe from prickle
Hue reminding thou of fervent fire
My eyes reflect on thy touch
A bouquet of red roses
A token of love from my heart

"Bouquet of Roses"
Tejashri Pathak

"French kisses in the deepest places

Delight shown on our faces"

Passion in our blood
Swallowing slowly my flood
Witnessing my explosion
Infected me with his love poison

Powerless against his spell
Kisses from hell
Passionate lover
Ecstasy we felt all over

Stripping me with his eyes
Doing anything he advise
Thrusting deeper than before
Devouring each other on the floor

Moaning as he goes deep inside
Emotions our guide
Enveloping him with my legs
In a Spanish voice he begs

Tongues meet
Dividing my thighs as he begun to eat
From my Caribbean ocean
Sliding into my tight potion

Steamy atmosphere
Seducing my soul multiple times a year
Savoring every taste
Wet kisses around my waist

Lustful thoughts bloom
Intoxicating me with his fume
Hearts pounding from pleasure
Rear entry I treasure

His tongue motions make me lose my mind
Whisper's elegantly from behind
Parting my red sea
Submissive plea

Painting my body with his tongue
Shedding his insecurities since young
His and her bed sheets of come in
Sharing our juices from within

Fingers around his knob
Both our hearts throb
Gently gliding his fingers
His cologne lingers

French kisses in the deepest places
Delight shown on our faces
Soaking in delight
Vampire bite

Fingers warmed between my cleavage
Enticing me to drink his leakage
The shape of his form
Quickly transform

Magical affection
Amazing connection
Kiss of enchantment
Sexual entrapment

Connected spiritually
Opened up physically
Deadly temptation
Desiring stimulation

Entering with satisfaction
Inner and outer attraction
Favorite medicine of affection
Instructions of multiple injections

"Arched in Pleasure"
Keisha Molby-Baez

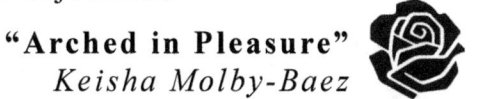

"Floating on a scallop shell to the island of Cyprus."

A bewitching beauty
Who one cannot resist looking at,
Sets off the fire of love
Along the path she walks.
Descended from the ancient Greeks,
Aphrodite holds the key to the locks of everyone's
      heart.
Ruling over the kingdom of beauty,
She appeared out of the foam of the sea,
Floating on a scallop shell to the island of Cyprus.

A sensational beauty, who everyone desires to have,
She is known as the lady of Cyprus.
Wielding the sword of beauty,
She was a powerful immortal deity,
Capable of stirring up romance among gods and
    mortals.
Born to Zeus and Dione,
She was a second-generation Olympian goddess.
Known in Roman mythology as Venus,
Her beauty leaves us all speechless.

"The Divine Beauty"
Rithika

"Your actions, the way they spell out love."

Your complexion, a sweet roasted caramel.
Your skin, rough like concrete; you can tell a lot from
    a man's hands (especially with a firm
    handshake).
Your eyes, innocent but not inexperienced.
Your actions, the way they spell out love.

Better defined as *hard work* so when you become my
　　　chauffeur,
and my masseuse,
and my chef,
and my best friend...
the best part of it is you do it because you want to,
　　　not because you have to.
And I'm with you because I want to. Not because I
　　　have to.

　　　　　　　　　　　　　　　"Volition"
　　　　　　　　　　　　　　Michel M. Antoine

"Having your love is the Fulfillment of my reason to live..."

Abolishment of the darkness
With the passionate love
Devour scent of your soul
Rebirth for the Reproduction of desires
Having your love is the Fulfillment of my reason to
    live
Still having the patience to virtue the love forever

Abolishment of the darkness,
Positive Approach
Feelings Reincarnate
Soul Harmony
Heart Symphony

With the passionate love
Angelic Eyes
Mesmerizing Beauty
Honey Voice
Velvet Fingers

Devour scent of your soul
Lips Entwined
Desire Igniting
Champagne Session
Craving Body

Reproduction of Emotions
Shadow Dancing
Enjoying Raining
Dusk Dawn
Love Humming

Having your love is the Fulfillment of my reason to
    live
Soul Reflection
Longing Awakens
You're Destiny
You're Pride

Still having the patience to virtue
The love forever
Happiness Together
Two Souls
One Body
Stay Forever

"Untitled #4"
Mahesh Maheshwari

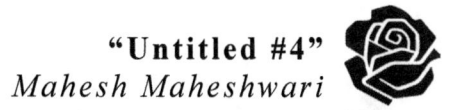

"Abolish your limitations and fear in commitments..."

A passionate mind is searching for ways to be
    captivated
With each step, discover or rediscover your passion.
The heat of passion in love—
Excitement and fulfilment only intensifies.
Abolish your limitations and fear in commitments,
Value the time, Value the love,
Value the relationship, Value the partner

Be blinded by love, love forever, be in love and be
    loved.
Have patience. Good things will occur.
Devour your intimacy—
A passionate love making satisfies the desire.
Love is ubiquitous and eternal
For it truly brings ardour, intimacy,
Memories, and reproduction.

"Blinded By Your Love"
Rama Barathi

"Past and present lost, replaced with laughter and light..."

My darling, how can I begin to describe you
Full of wondrous contradictions
Endearing you to me without thought or conscious
    action

Eyes of blue, lost in waves of cerulean
Willfully swimming deeper into their depths
Drowning sweetly in the deep

Hands rough from work, captivating
The feel of callus and strength against petal soft skin
Igniting and alighting the imagination

Catching a glimpse of soul, locked in gaze
Innocent movements capturing interest
The slightest catch of bated breath

Titian hair, refracting thousands of blazing lights
Sinking fingers and shifting strands
Closing eyes and soft sighs filter the air

Beneath the surface, steadfast vitality
Lies stunning gentility and compassion
Letting go of prized catch for the sake of life

Never one to make an easy chase, hardships taking
        toll
Assuaging fear with astounding patience
Soothing a frightened girl without machination

Past and present lost, replaced with laughter and light
Velvet tones and hushed rumbles
Quiet thunderstorm rolling in the night

Curious, how your beautiful mind spins
Searching for answers the world cannot provide for
        you
Finding your own path towards resplendent
        understanding

With you, the fear disappears
Glimmering hope appears and dazzles
Sublime dreams coming alive in our waking world

"Adrift"
Michaela Jean

"Bewitching mysterious puzzle

Even Gods couldn't decipher"

Born from the union of
Powerful celestial entities
Pearl beauty emerging from
Foamy waves of roaring ocean
With a scent of red roses
Adolescent goddess of pleasure
A seductive symbol of love

Bewitching mysterious puzzle
Even Gods couldn't decipher
An immortal proof of paradox
A deity dressed in soulful love
Hiding a dark curse of revenge
Goddess of fertility giving birth
To inspiration and longing
O Aphrodite, cast a magnetic spell
To turn my words into love songs

"Hymn for Aphrodite"
Tejashri Pathak

"The red satin slip contours her shapely body creating an internal fire."

She feels sexy when she wears it,
Seductive and full of passionate desire;
The red satin slip contours her shapely body, creating
    an internal fire.
Lips juicy and plump ready to be united with those of
    her lovers—
With each kiss, Garnet colored lipstick stains his lips,
    neck, and collar.

Motivated by the gesture to come a little closer,
A red nail polished finger suggests it with one lustful motion.
Awaiting the lovebirds are red roses and red wine on ice,
Decadent chocolates, Netflix, and chilling during this quarantine definitely sounds about right...
Music softly playing in the background by Lyfe Jennings, must be nice (sing along).

"The Lady in Red"
LaDasha-Diamond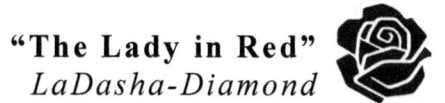

"We are each

The savoury and the sweetness

Constituting different parts"

Falling in love
Literal piece of cake
Staying in love
Hardest part

Being best friends
Felt comfortable
Very reliable
Further flourished

Meaningful relationship
Like cheese
Only better with time
Like wine
Delicious in time

Definitely not
A concoction of paradoxes
Absolutely
A combination of
Happiness and forgiveness

Time passes
Both mature
Never feeling
Like we give too much
Nor receiving too little

Mutual understanding
Unconditional love
Far from burdensome
Both respectful of boundaries

We are each
The savory and the sweetness
Constituting different parts
Of a whole

Both communicating
What we need
Never expecting
Most important
Sharing similar end-goals
Aligned to one another

Mutual acknowledgment of flaws
Enjoying time alone
Taking pleasure in our own presence
Accepting each other
Exactly the way we are

Supporting and receiving
One another's positive energy
Enjoying our differences
Flourishing through nourishment
Mutual engagement

Increased levels
Giving and receiving
A universal agreement of supply
Without any demands

Both our lips
Speaking only truth
Reading in-between the lines
Our flesh approves our ties

Unconditional giving and receiving
A mutual union of
I got you and you got me
We are a true example of
Opposites attract

He's bars and I'm lounges
He's movies and I'm books
He's jokes and I'm smiles
He's tunes and I'm lyrics
He's insecure and I'm confident
He's beer and I'm wine

A unique combination of
Mutual supply and demand
An agreement built on unselfish love
A union that demands nothing
Yet supplies everything

"Supply and Demand After Falling in Love"
Keisha Molby-Baez

"Love is a two-way road
Which is always under construction."

Love is a two-way road
Which is always under construction.
I first saw her at a party,
Going all out on the dance floor.
Her elegant style with swanky moves captivated me.
Dance is a poem,
In which the movements are its words.
Dance seemed to pull us closer
Into the beautiful world of love.
From then, everything took place in a flash.
After knowing each other for three years,
I went down on my knees
To catch the moon of my night.

Every morning, I woke up with her sweet hugs
And every second with her relished my life.
Dancing at nights with her,
My hands closed in hers,
Wrapped in expanses of furs,
I realised that she was a connoisseur who perfectly
    understood the art of love.
When I felt low, I always felt a soft, warm touch on
    my shoulder which said, "I'm here for you"
The ring on her finger, filled with my love,
Was powerful enough to keep away hungry women
    predators.
My voice was the ultimate medicine of her sorrow.
I may not be her king,
But I'm the prince who has come to steal away my
    princess's heart and keep it along with me
    forever!

"The Art of Love"
Rithika

"Your eyes devoured me completely
By waving a magical wand..."

I never believed in true love.
But when I looked deep into your eyes,
With a powerful force,
It pulled me into the
Deepest passion of love.
Your eyes devoured me completely
By waving a magical wand,
That no one could see;
Abolishing all my beliefs, limits,
Policies, and philosophies,
I fell in love with you.

Every time I see the same warmth
In your eyes,
My love attains fulfillment.
I have enough patience,
To live in silence with the
Thoughts about you
Reproducing my feelings for you
And being in love with you,
Until my last breath.
Because my love is unconditional;
That was found deep into your eyes.

"Deep Into Your Eyes"
Chandini

"Recognizing the twin flame
Craving the connection"

Emotion overflowing my heart
Yearning to share
Wanting to fill the empty spaces

Recognizing a twin flame
Craving the connection
Almost demanding the same devotion

Needing to fill the broken spaces with his love
Coveting the small moments
Insisting on cherishing the little things

Possessing a need to care for him
To be everything he needs
Without taking away from myself

To pour myself into every aspect of us
To find a partner that accepts my attentions
To love and be equally loved in return

How is it possible to feel so deeply
Oh, my love, if you could feel as deeply as I do
Rampant hope springs from long dry wells

"Hope Springs"
Michaela Jean

"All your queen demands of you in return is your support."

I'd love you more than anything in this world,
All I demand of you in return is your care.
I'd sacrifice anything for you,
All I demand of you in return is your honesty.
I'd do anything for the sake of your happiness,
All I demand of you in return is your attention.
I'd share every bit of my heart with you,
All I demand of you in return is your trust.
I'd leave even my attitude for you,
All I demand of you in return is your love.

I'd give myself completely to you,
All I demand of you in return is your loyalty.
I'd face any kind of predicament for you,
All I demand of you in return is your
Warmth and protection.
I'd build a beautiful castle called family for you, my
    king,
All your queen demands of you in return is your
    support.
I'd give away my everything for you,
All I demand of you in return is to be your
Everything forever.

"Supply and Demand"
Chandini

"Love is to love from the soul

Love is simple Love"

Love is knowing each other
Love is selfless
Love is togetherness
Love is full of emotions
Love is to love from the soul
Love is simply Love

Love is knowing each other
Spending time
Dancing together
Undescribed desires
Helping each other

Love is selfless
No expectation
Pure love
Feelings awaken
Pain heals

Love is togetherness
Crossing hurdles
Lovely cuddles
Singing riddles
Nothing hinders

Love is full of emotions
Heart melting
Sunshine shimmering
Stars dancing
Longing igniting

Love is to love from the soul
Not Lust
Soul connection
Heart Symphony
Soul Harmony

Love is simply Love
Makes us
Breath Together
Love Eternal
Stay Forever

"Untitled #5"
Mahesh Maheshwari
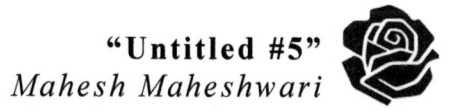

AUTHORS

"Behind every poem are words. Behind those words are people."

Chandini is an 18-year-old aspiring doctor. Her positive and compassionate demeanor, in addition to her passion for people, fuels her desire to help those that she is able to assist. She is dedicated to her friends and her family, whom she loves dearly. Though she is working towards fulfilling her dream of being a doctor, Chandini is an artist at heart and thoroughly enjoys indulging in many disciplines including, writing, singing, and drawing. She has been fond of writing since she was little and is excited to now be part of the Poetix University family. If you want to see more of her artistic work musings, follow her on Instagram at @chandu_bublee.

Dhruvil Purani is an India based writer who enjoys writing poetry, blogs, and quotes. He is currently pursuing his Bachelor's Degree in Electrical Engineering, but that doesn't stop him from indulging in journal writing and sketching. Dhruvil began writing in 2017 and primarily writes about mental health and love. He has been published in several anthologies including *Clogged Impression*s published by Spectrum of Thoughts, *Stardust* published by Fanatixx Publications, *Mirakee* published by Mirakee Publication, and *BLEED* Anthology by Poetix University. You can connect with Dhruvil on Instagram at @shades_n_sayings and read his blogs at http://blogsbydap.wordpress.com

James Dean River also known as The Dean of Poetry, is an author, spoken word artist, and YouTuber who resides in Brooklyn, New York. Through his words, he promotes positivity and inspiration. He shares life lessons in hopes of bettering the lives of his audience. James has been writing since he was 14 years old and he published his book *Words From The Heart* in 2018. He also holds a Bachelor's Degree in Business Science from Brooklyn College. The Dean of Poetry lives to inspire the world one moment at a time. James can be found across all social media platforms, you only have to look him up by his name and you will find him.

Keisha Molby-Baez, also known by her poet name Coco, is a writer, author, veteran, curator, mother of three, and a Bronx coordinator. Keisha is the author of two self-empowering poetry books *Tears laced with Fire* and *A little bit of Sugar*. Her poem "Seeds Planted" is published and featured in *MER VOX* Quarterly. Keisha's poems are anthologized in *Inside the Panic Room, United: Volume Red, BX Writers* and *The Revolution*, of which she is a *Pushcart Prize* nominee. Keisha is an incredible supporter and producer of her community. She has a lovely inner light and a raw-truth style that captivates her audience. She is the creator of *Coco's Delight* and dedicated to her life path of turning pain into purpose. She enjoys performing, challenging herself, and empowering others. Keisha is currently working on her third book and next project.

LaDasha-Diamond is a community leader and artist who uses her own struggles and journey of self-determination to inspire individual and community resilience. Her work focuses on healing trauma so we can triumph and reclaim our ability to dream.

Mahesh (King) Maheshwari, is a passionate new writer from Delhi. He holds an MBA and works in the entertainment industry, but it was heartbreak that helped him realize his gift with words. Mahesh primarily writes about romance, pain, darkness, and brokenness, with hopes of being the voice for the people who are not able to express their feelings surrounding love or suffering. Despite the heavy content of his writing, he is a jovial person and is quite easy to approach thanks to his calm and kind demeanor. He is an upcoming writer that you should keep an eye on, and to do that, you can follow him on Instagram at @kingthoughts2303.

Michaela Jean, known as Mickiejean, is a writer from the heart of the Midwest, born and raised in Denver, Colorado. She is a loving fur mom to two adorable bunnies, Smokey and Jasper, in which one unfortunately crossed the rainbow bridge. She fell out of love with writing for quite a while but recently rekindled her passion and love for the art. She draws inspiration from her fur kids, nature, and the beauty of her home state. From the rumbling late summer thunderstorms to the quiet white winters that blanket the Rockies, she is planning on releasing a novel within the next year and is excited to take the journey.

Michel M. Antoine is a bilingual Licensed Mental Health Counselor, dancer, Zumba instructor, poet, and author. She self-published her first book: *STOP, LOVE, and LISTEN* in December of 2018. This collection of poems and journal entries is a self-healing journey that focuses on self-love and taking your time in all life aspects. She has also been published in two anthologies. She writes to express her emotions and heal from traumatic experiences. She encourages writing as a healing tool for all.

Nupur Nair, also known as 'The Dancing Ink' was born in India and raised in Dubai. While Nupur received her degree in Graphic Communication and Illustration from Loughborough University she has been in love with the written word for as long as she can remember. Nupur enjoys exploring a number of topics through her writing including mental health, nature, love, and the varying types of relationships people find themselves in. She utilizes different techniques and styles to enhance her writing like Japanese poetry, sonnets, acrostics, blackout poems, etc. Nupur feels most accomplished when she is able to connect and relate to others through her writing. She has been published in the *Tears of Swords* Anthology by Poets Tribe and Poets Globe, and *BLEED* Anthology by Poetix University (both available on Amazon). You can connect with Nupur on Instagram at @thedancingink.

Rama Barathi is an Economics PhD Scholar at the University of Madras, India. Since childhood she aspired to become a writer, singer, and a teacher. She loves to do a lot of charity work and travelling is her primary interest. She began writing at the age of nine. She has lived and studied in different countries. She has published many of her writings in the Times of India newspaper. She took part in a NASA contest, submitted a poem holding 336 lines and has received rewards. She also is an active tutor for spoken English, economics, drawing & painting and music. She is a 26-year-old and holds eight educational degrees apart from her PhD. In her words, she writes because that's the best way to communicate something to this world when speaking doesn't help. Rama writes poems to show what she feels, and her passion is to become a writer.

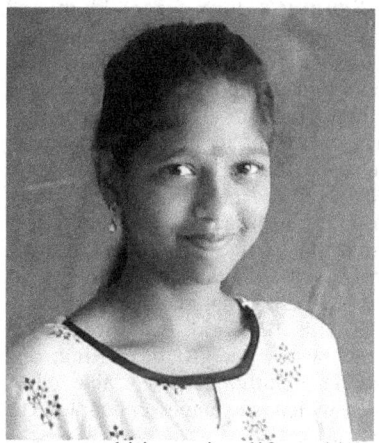

Rashmi is a 15-year-old from India who is currently pursuing her higher studies. She has been writing for the past seven years, when schoolwork permitted. Her participation in various school competitions helped her realize that she is quite an impressive writer of poems and short stories. It was in partaking in workshops and competitions that led Rashmi to discover that writing is truly one of her greatest passions. Writing enables Rashmi to express her emotions, broaden her perspectives and think outside of the box while exploring various genres and subject matters. In her opinion, writing is a form of art wherein our pen becomes the brush. Rashmi has many ambitions in life which includes writing as much as possible and to have it all published. Her work will be featured in an upcoming anthology. Her writings can be seen on Instagram at @My_.dialect.

Rithika, who is 15 years old and from India, has been writing for the past four years. As an only child looking for ways to avoid loneliness, she started entertaining herself by exploring the craft of writing. She is skilled at and passionate about the written word spanning across several genres including poetry, short stories, and essays. Rithika sees poetry as a communication language which allows the poets to communicate and share their feelings with words when they don't have anybody to listen to them. One of her goals in life is to become a published author and poet. Her work will be featured in an upcoming anthology. You can read more of her poetry on Instagram at @poetry._craze.

Sarrah Safi believes that words are her calling/ language/ expression. She fell in love with writing at an early age and never stopped. Her ambition led to a writing career (politics, cannabis, health, medicine, business, etc.). But in April of 2020, the Poetix Bleed Challenge re-introduced her to the calling her soul was aching to express poetry. She found a way to look at her past trauma and make sense of it. Shortly after, she signed up their Roses Workshop and wrote romantic poetry for the first time that helped polish her relationship with her husband. Now she continues to write from her soul's perspective while living her best life in Colorado with her family.

Shana Bennett's love for children and heart for people led her to pursue and obtain a Bachelors in Psychology, a Masters in Social Work and her current career as a school counselor at an elementary school in New York. Outside of her professional career, Shana released her first book of poetry in 2018 titled *Trenched Treasures (available on Amazon)*. This book is a compilation of poetry written over the course of a decade seeking to inspire herself and others to see their gifts as treasures of value that need not be hidden but shared with the world. It is through her professional work, her gift of writing, and her work via her church that she is able to live her purpose which is to empower people to be their best selves, break the chains of injustice in our society, and restore individuals and communities to the way God intended.

Sharron Green from Surrey in South East England describes herself as a menopausal empty nester. As @Rhymes_n_Roses on Instagram, she enjoys sharing her poetry which combines nostalgia and attempts to make sense of modern life. Although many of her subjects are serious, she tries to inject humour and positivity. Sharron has self-published a book of rhymes titled, *Introducing Rhymes_n_Roses*, and will soon have poems in six other international anthologies.

Taneeka L. Wilder is a self-published author of *On the Precipice of Love Illuminated*. Taneeka uses her words to penetrate and nourish hearts for the purpose of healing, inspiration, and reflection. She has been interviewed on Progressive Radio PRN. FM, LiveHip-Hop Daily, and was also featured on the radio program Midnight Meditations with CharLena, and Mike Geffner's Inspired Word NYC. Taneeka has performed at various venues, and facilitated workshops on health, wellness, and healing. She is currently envisioning her next literary venture, with a second book in progress.

Tejashri Pathak is an electronics engineer by day and an accidental poet by night. She is from a small town in Maharashtra, India. She completed her Masters in Engineering and worked as an assistant professor in an engineering college. While writing her research papers and thesis, she realised she could do something special with words. Tejashri's journey started with scribbled words in her journal and it took her three years to actually start taking poetry writing seriously. She loves to convey raw emotions through poetry. Currently, she is planning to publish a book of her poems and her future plans include writing a fiction novel. Tejashri shares her creations on Instagram at @soul_lost_in_poetry_.

INDEX

L

Aphrodite's Release - Shana Bennett	2
Like A Rose - James Dean Rivera	4
Supply and Demand - Nupur Nair	6
Highway to Love - Dhruvil Purani	8
The Girl in Red - Rithika	10
Red Rendezvous - Nupur Nair	12
The Demand and Supply in Our Love - Rama Barathi	14
My Romeo - Chandini	16
Shower of Love - Dhruvil Purani	18
Lost, At Sea - Sharron Green	20
Willing Womb - Shana Bennett	22
Her Beauty in Red - Rashmi	24
It Was Fall - Shana Bennett	26
Culinary & Candy - Taneeka L. Wilder	30
Red Love - Dhruvil Purani	32

O

A P H R O D I T E - Sharron Green	36
Aphrodite's Power - James Dean Rivera	37
Aphrodite: An Ode - Sarrah Safi	38
Leap of Faith - Michaela Jean	40
Love in Red, Unrequited Love - Mahesh Maheshwari	42
Since You Left - Rithika	44
Untitled #1 - Michel M. Antoine	46
Supporting Actor - Tejashri Pathak	48
Come Back To Me, My Love - Rama Barathi	50
Don't Deny the Reaper - Michaela Jean	52
Rewind - Sarrah Safi	54
Untitled #2 - Mahesh Maheshwari	56
When I saw him… - Rashmi	58
My Broken Soul - Chandini	60
Monochrome Keys of Love - Tejashri Pathak	62
The Message - Taneeka L. Wilder	64

V

Where did you go? - Rashmi	68
Lost Love I Say Not - Taneeka L. Wilder	70
Daring to Resuscitate - Shana Bennett	72
Driving Myself Crazy - Michel M. Antoine	76
What is 'Love'? - Nupur Nair	78
The Most Beautiful of Them All - LaDasha-Diamond	80
One More Try - Keisha Molby-Baez	82
Two Conversations - James Dean Rivera	86
Red - Michel M. Antoine	88
At First Glance - James Dean Rivera	90
Love in Red - Sharron Green	92
Aphrodite: A Bronx Tale - Taneeka L. Wilder	94
Yours - Nupur Nair	96
Hot Sand On My Beach - Keisha Molby-Baez	98
Untitled #3 - LaDasha-Diamond	102

E

Sensation - Sarrah Safi	*106*
My Mystery Man - Rama Barathi	*108*
A Bouquet of Roses - Tejashri Pathak	*110*
Arched in Pleasure - Keisha Molby-Baez	*112*
The Divine Beauty - Rithika	*114*
Volition - Michel M. Antoine	*116*
Untitled #4 - Mahesh Maheshwari	*118*
Blinded by Your Love - Rama Barathi	*120*
Adrift - Michaela Jean	*122*
Hymn for Aphrodite - Tejashri Pathak	*124*
The Lady in Red - LaDasha-Diamond	*126*
Supply and Demand After Falling in Love - Keisha Molby-Baez	*128*
The Art of Love - Rithika	*132*
Deep Into Your Eyes - Chandini	*134*
Hope Springs - Michaela Jean	*136*
Supply and Demand - Chandini	*138*
Untitled #5 - Mahesh Maheshwari	*140*

"Love is the ultimate journey."

-tonii